44031

I Bet You Didn't Know That ...

YOU CAN'T SINK IN THE DEAD SEA

and Other Facts and Curiosities

YOU CAN'T SINK IN THE DEAD SEA

by Carol Iverson • pictures by Jack Lindstrom

Lerner Publications Company • Minneapolis

*With thanks to Gary DeGrote and his sixth graders,
Addi Engen, Isabel Marvin, Joan Ennis, Torild
Homstad, and my husband, Art.*

Copyright © 1990 by Lerner Publications Company

Library of Congress Cataloging-in-Publication Data

Iverson, Carol.
    You can't sink in the Dead Sea and other facts and curiosities /
Carol Iverson ; pictures by Jack Lindstrom
        p.   cm. – (I bet you didn't know that)
    Summary: Presents a variety of miscellaneous geographical,
historical, and cultural facts about different parts of the world.
      ISBN 0-8225-2278-0 (lib. bdg.)
    1. Curiosities and wonders – Juvenile literature. [1. Curiosities
and wonders.] I. Lindstrom, Jack, Ill. II. Title. III. Series:
Iverson, Carol. I bet you didn't know that.
AG243.I85   1990
030 – dc20   89-27183
                                                               CIP
                                                               AC

Manufactured in the United States of America

1   2   3   4   5   6   7   8   9   10   99   98   97   96   95   94   93   92   91   90

I Bet You Didn't Know That...

People weigh less if they are standing at the equator than they do if they are standing at the North or South pole.

I Bet You Didn't Know That...

People weigh less at the top of a mountain than they do at sea level.

In 1867, the United States bought Alaska from Russia for $7,200,000, or about two cents an acre.

At their closest points, the United States and the Soviet Union are just over two miles (three kilometers) apart.

MOSCOW 4000 Mi.

The coldest inhabited place in the world is the Siberian village of Oymyakon, where temperatures have reached −96°F (−71°C).

It is sometimes colder in New York City than it is in Iceland.

Australia is the only country that is also a continent.

NEW YORK 4000 MI.

I Bet You Didn't Know That...

The most valuable paper currency in the United States was the $100,000 bill. It bore a picture of President Woodrow Wilson.

The motto on one of the first U.S. coins was "Mind Your Business."

The cacao bean, which is used to make chocolate and cocoa, was once used by the Aztec Indians both as a coin and a beverage source.

The world's first coin was made in Lydia, in Asia Minor, in about 650 B.C.

The Chinese were the first people to use paper money – in around A.D. 600.

The yo-yo was originally
a weapon used in the
Philippine jungles.

9

I Bet You Didn't Know That...

The "chewing gum locket" was manufactured in 1889. It was designed so a person could carry chewing gum without it getting dirty.

The oldest known map was drawn on a clay tablet. It showed northern Mesopotamia around 3800 B.C.

The earliest known playing cards were made in China.

The novel *Les Miserables* by Victor Hugo contains a sentence that is 823 words long.

In December 1961, it was discovered that a painting by Matisse in New York's Museum of Modern Art was hanging upside down.

The longest film ever made premiered in 1970. It ran for 48 hours and was titled *The Longest, Most Meaningless Movie in the World.*

I Bet You Didn't Know That...

In some parts of Mexico, soap was once used as money.

At one time, North American Indians of the Pacific coast used blankets for money.

Flat, round stones weighing hundreds of pounds were once used as money by the Yap Islanders in the Pacific.

Alexander the Great was the first person to be pictured on a coin.

Franklin Delano Roosevelt's portrait was placed on the U.S. dime because of his association with the March of Dimes charity.

Ridges were put on the edges of coins to discourage people from shaving off bits of gold and silver.

I Bet You Didn't Know That...

All race horses become one year older on New Year's Day, no matter when they were born.

It is a Korean tradition that on a child's first birthday, a table is filled with various objects. Whatever the child picks up first is a sign of his or her future: threads mean long life, coins mean riches, and a pencil, which is considered the best, means a literary life.

If you lived on planet Mercury, you could celebrate your birthday every 88 days, since it takes 88 Earth-days for Mercury to orbit the Sun.

Summers on Uranus are 21 Earth-years long.

I Bet You Didn't Know That...

The model for the Indian head penny was the engraver's daughter.